Let Your Love Be Contagious

Keyonna A Monroe

3G Publishing, Inc.
4495 Atlanta Highway, Suite C28
Loganville, GA 30052
www.3gpublishinginc.com

©2020, Keyonna A. Monroe. All rights reserved.

No part of this book may be reproduced, stored in a retrieval system, or transmitted by any means without the written permission of the author.

First published by 3G Publishing, Inc., June, 2020.

Printed in the United States of America

ISBN: 9781941247723

Because of the dynamic nature of the Internet, any web addresses or links contained in this book may have changed since publication and may no longer be valid. The views expressed in this work are solely those of the author and do not necessarily reflect the views of the publisher, and the publisher hereby disclaims any responsibility for them.

Dedicated to the kids in my nonprofit organization.
Thanks for learning to love yourself first #LYF
so that you can give it to others freely and abundantly.

Let your love be contagious

Deja que tu amor sea contagioso

Let it start from within

Deja que comience desde adentro

Love doesn't care where you live

Al amor no le importa donde vives

nor the color of your skin

ni el color de tu piel

It is kind, it is patient, it is full of generosity

Es amable, es paciente, está lleno de generosidad

to every girl and every boy
Para cada niña y cada niño

Give your love to your friends

Dale tu amor a tus amigas y amigos

Let your love be contagious
Share it even with your pets

Deja que tu amor sea contagioso
Compártelo incluso con tus mascotas

Because animals need love too
Make sure to give with no regrets

Porque los animales también necesitan amor
Asegúrate de dar sin remordimientos

Then you're always in good standing
With the One who first loved you.

Entonces siempre estás al día
Con el que primero te amó.

El Fin

www.ingramcontent.com/pod-product-compliance
Lightning Source LLC
Chambersburg PA
CBHW041433040426

42451CB00023B/3499